AF361223

A

DEBUT

COLLECTION

FROM

serena morrigan

A Song for Every Scar

First Printing, 2021

Printing information available on the last page.

ISBN-13: 978-3-9823098-0-4 (sc)

ISBN-13: 978-3-9823098-1-1 (eb)

Co-Editors: Brooke Goodwin & Ada Holm

Book & Logo Design: Dot Ink Creative

Serena Morrigan
c/o AutorenServices.de
Birkenallee 24
D–36037 Fulda

A Song for Every Scar

poetry collection

I am more than my pain

But I am mostly my pain

It doesn't define me – yet

It taints everything I do

My naïve brain was built

From trauma I endured

It's so much work to rewire

When serotonin's hard to come by

I am made of memories

I buried within my soul

But they're ready to attack

Flashing before my eyes

I dug my rabbit hole

And down I go, endlessly

Spiralling out of control

Farther away from reality

for

chester

TABLE OF CONTENTS

Intro

I – XI

Songs of Obsidian Ink

12 – 37

Songs of Crimson Turmoil

38 – 59

Songs of Magnolia Disorder

60 – 101

TABLE OF CONTENTS

Songs of Lavender Sorrow

102 – 137

Songs of Cerulean Misery

138 – 157

Songs of Emerald Hope

158 – 177

Outro

178 – 181

SONGS OF

Obsidian Ink

*"Let me paint a picture with
these words burning like magma
under my volcano skin."*

autumn's in the air

It's a typewriter kind of day

When the sky is grey

And the leaves are falling

All I need is a piece of paper

And a hot cup of tea

My mind dancing euphorically

To the clicking & clacking

Of the keys telling my story

diary of chaos

What if I could just spill my emotions

Onto the paper like black ink, irremovable

And keep them in a diary of chaos

Releasing the pain and shame I've felt

And every mistake I've ever made

So I could keep all the happiness in my heart

And look to the future with a smile on my face

If I could capture my sorrow on paper

I wouldn't do anything else but write

awake forever

How useless are these words

If they can't describe the state I'm in?

It's been a weird couple of hours

Unannounced

i n s o m n i a

Came knocking on my door again

And declared that she is here to stay

It's been 48 hours and more is to come

I've long surrendered to her calls

awake forever

Awake forever, I'll spend my days

Sipping tea and writing lines

Awake forever, I'll spend my nights

Staring at the sky & cursing those stars

A zombie pacing for all eternity

unsent letter

All the words I didn't say

I write them down for you

I cannot break these chains that keep

My soul from flowing free

Instead, I take this pen in hand

To show you what I mean

I slowly watch the courage seep

Through cracks I used to seal

imperfection

There's beauty in the imperfect

The crumpled-up pages, the blacked out letters

Reminding you life is a canvas

And there's no opaque white to gloss over scars

And mistakes are part of the process

Opportunities to learn & grow

The utopia we so desperately seek

Is merely an illusion, trying

To make sense of the inevitability

Of falling over and over again

my volcano skin

Let me paint a picture

With these words

Burning like magma

Under my volcano skin

They hold the anger

I don't tell you about

Only when my pen hits the paper

Can I express the pain

I so carefully hide behind 'I'm fine'

And so I lay them down to rest

The glowing embers of my being

For you to read instead

escape

Words come knocking

From within my rib cage

Looking for an escape

D o n ' t   t h e y   k n o w ?

There's another way out

Other than through

My chest with a dagger

everything is poetry

One day when I'll look back at

This moment in time

Everything will be poetry

Every word I read & wrote

An extraordinary journey

Iridescent treasure chest

Full of sacred memories

And I'm not sure if I'll be able to

Listen to their voices

The same way ever again

these poems cut like broken glass

These poems cut like broken glass

I cannot keep away from the allure

Opening doors to the subconscious

Reliving all the painful memories

For the sake of purging these thoughts

Unhelpful, unhealthy, unnecessary

I keep repeating the same old lines

These words are a knife in my hand

Tracing the stitches across my heart

Someone save me from myself

like dust in the sunlight

Two good days in a row

And suddenly I don't know

What to write about anymore

So I let the keys guide me

To remind me of the words

That used to float about

Like dust in the sunlight

pearl necklace

I feel creativity flowing through my veins

It's a funny feeling, this need to create

Even if it isn't meant for the world to see

It's cathartic to spill it onto paper

To get these pictures out of my head

And pour everything into these images

A bottomless pit of metaphors & similes

I thread words like pearls on a string

And wear them around my neck without fear

This time I will let honesty take the reins

everything about me is a lie

I don't think I've ever been myself

But I don't recognise the woman

In the mirror looking back at me

Anymore; I've built a wall of poetry

Protecting me from reality

I locked the truth in cold cement

And painted the bricks with fantasy

everything about me is a lie

I don't know if I have changed

Or if I'm merely pretending to be

The person you see between the lines

Carving out dreams & destinies

I am not who you think I am

But please don't tear it all down

Don't wake me from this dream

I crafted from what I had left to give

• A TANKA •

on writing in winter

A piece of paper

Coffee in the candlelight

Thoughts dripping like wax

Another moment in time

Looking for answers in ink

the vocabulary

If I stare at this blank page long enough

Words just slip out, I'm creating something

I don't know where they even come from

Why is my mind making up words?

Words that aren't even my own, it seems

When did they find their way in here?

Oh, I know, everything leads back to you

You taught me the vocabulary I needed

To express how traumatic this life has been

If this is my purpose, then thank you

soul language

This is my soul's language, brutally honest & raw

My actual voice might use other sounds & syllables

But the voice inside is made up of these words

Ethereal truths tingling under my proverbial tongue

Not to be said out loud, but to be read instead

There's just no other way to express these thoughts

soul language

Gnawing away at the fabric of my mind like moths

So I type them out on paper, black ink printed

Letter by letter, taking up space, spilling a canvas

Cleansing my soul of decrepit phrases spiralling

That lingered for far too long under the surface

The words were always there, now let me use them

islands of pure imagination

Holding words like embers

Scorching my palms with ease

I eventually had to let them go

The ink flowing like lava

Slowly, but steadily creating

Islands of pure imagination

Coming to life, one word at a time

the silver lining

What is it about the early morning hours

That turns my mind into a river flowing

The words pouring out like a waterfall

Ideas rushing through my brain unstoppable

Is it the cool breeze after a hot summer's day?

Or the cosiness of the candlelight in December?

All I know is this insomnia is a blessing & a curse

For the night is not as treasured as the day

i break my own heart

When will they notice?

I write poetry to break my own heart

To relive the trauma in times of calm

I feel alive only when I grieve

So I write and weave strings of heartache

Into the very verses I lay before you

ocean of words

Beneath an ocean of words I hide

For the truth is too much to bear

I'd rather drown in all these letters

Than shake them off my tongue

I've never learned the vocabulary

To express in ways other than this

For how long my soul's been on fire

And the reasons behind the flames

They'll never know the true extent

For my inner child remains confused

Lying on the bottom of the stormy sea

With mermaid lungs, she plays alone

when a poem knocks on my door

I'm sorry, but when a poem knocks on my door

I have to let it in and offer some tea & biscuits

I'm hospitable like that sometimes when it's urgent

It's that one friend you never liked, but I'll invite her anyway

We'll make morbid jokes and talk about death

And all the other things people remain silent about

Those that make you feel uncomfortable in the sunlight

I'm sorry, but when a poem knocks on my door

I have to drop everything and welcome in the darkness

poetry heart

This poetry heart of mine is fragile

Handle it with care, the paper's torn

Soaked in lukewarm coffee and tears

It's all a poet really needs these days

To extract the essence of emotions

Spilling poems onto wooden floors

A stage for the beautifully cracked pieces

That no gold in the world can mend

But the hearts of the similarly broken

SONGS OF

Crimson Turmoil

*"How I carved marble veins
into this skin, inspired by
the white cliffs of Thassos."*

cautionary tale

Three years old and you already notice

My arms look different, something's off

But I can't possibly explain to you

How I carved marble veins into this skin

Inspired by the white cliffs of Thassos

Where I had spent a summer in trance

Swallowing mistakes like rubies

To pour them into marmoreal moulds

cautionary tale

Sculpting crimson trails of release

Future lost in the back of my mind

I never thought I'd be so afraid

That explaining all of this to you

May result in the past repeating itself

Let me be the cautionary tale they tell

Of a girl entrapped & turned to marble

On an island in a far-away land

frozen in time

A look in the mirror reveals

I seem older, subtle lines

Wrap around my tired eyes

Slowly, my hair turns white

Before I know it, I will be snow

An ancient soul frozen in time

Holding onto my childish ways

When will I finally grow up?

i suffer alone

It's not even on purpose

I just feel safer

Keeping my pain to myself

In a world

Where everyone's a threat

With no one to turn to

So I learned to hide

To keep my emotions inside

Until I'm back in my room

Where I can

Suffer alone – it's okay

the final straw

Yesterday's wounds turned into today's scars

The pain is long gone, but the memory lives on

In the bruised perception of my mortal self

I throw stone after stone at the mirror in front of me

Your vicious words have carved out my heart

Filling my soul with lessons of hate & shame

This destruction has always been inevitable

The way you mocked me on my thirteenth birthday

The final straw I needed to break apart

rock bottom

I remember my first night

At the psychiatric hospital

After hitting rock bottom

Thinking, how did I get this low?

I must be insane to end up here

Safe from myself, locked away

It's nothing like the movies though

They actually tried to help me

But what's the point in getting help

If you just cannot accept it?

I was too young to see it then

And so I hit rock bottom again

on suicide watch

Like a criminal

I pace through my new home

A room, like a cell

Nothing inside to hurt me

There's no lock on my door

But the corridor is secured

By a double door system

I can't overcome

I wonder how I got here

72 hours to figure it out

And a quarter year later

I'll be back to square one

seventeen

On a mellow day in December

I spent my seventeenth birthday

Locked away in the psych ward

Because **that's where the cool kids party**

Unashamed, beaten, and broken

With the world on their shoulders

That's how you celebrate life and

Pending death in a padded cell

childhood trauma

Imagine what it was like

Growing up, dealing with this

I was struggling to survive

To hide the cuts, ashamed,

That so perfectly described

Growing up, dealing with this

All the trauma you didn't see

Postponing my reaction

To when I'm back in my room

To write another song

childhood trauma

Imagine what it was like

No one's taking you seriously

You are struggling alone

In a room full of rebels

Crying for their attention

No one's taking you seriously

When you grow up like this

Knowing this isn't just a phase

But clear-cut depression

Hitting like a ton of bricks

snippets of memories

Snippets of memories returning

Like your headphones and how

You always used to wear them

How these cuts stung in the shower

And how little I cared for them

Memories like that time we sang

A song we both loved to death

Because we hated that boy so much

It's like remembering the lyrics

To a song almost forgotten

As if no time had passed at all

Memories as clear as day

I thought I had lost them

coffee-stained letters

Coffee stains on the letters I never sent

I've tried to come up with so many clever words

The caffeine still running through my veins

Yet it's a futile fight to think it will change anything

I'm merely a shadow of what life's supposed to look like

And I feel at home among the monsters & ghosts

They raised the girl I am today

So I'll burn these letters along with the fallen leaves

Hoping for better days to come

in the moonlight

I glance at the moon

Shining in the distance

A familiar solitude

Expanding in my rib cage

This everlasting sombre state

Begs the blood to coagulate

I wonder what it must be like

in the moonlight

To live without words like these

Speaking of an abundance of

Trauma and survival

No matter where I am in life

The moon has always been

The one constant friend

Watching over me

Comforting the lonely child

In the darkest corner of my heart

sticks and stones

Sticks and stones don't break my bones

My skeleton's still intact

But all these vicious words you uttered

Hit deeper than anything you threw my way

An infantile mind open to contempt

Took all your verbal assaults carefully in

And slowly, over time, made them my own

Sealing the soul with scorching self-hate

It's a long road to recovery, to undo the damage

To take all these thoughts & throw them out

And let love seep through these cracks

sticks and stones

II

Sticks and stones don't break my bones

But you left wounds that still need to heal

not my fault

I forgive myself for mistakes I made

When I was a lost and lonely child

Too young, too innocent to know

How this society works, how life can be

A cruel place where monsters hide

It wasn't my fault I didn't fit in

Trying my best to appease the ones

Supposed to teach and protect me

distorted glass

Today I am full of love for my friends

Who think better of me than I do

My mind is a vicious place, you don't

Want to look outside these eyes

The mirror is distorted glass

Showing the demons inside my skull

Exactly what they want to see

Am I worthy to be called a friend

When I feel like I'm constantly on fire?

Why can't I be kind for once

To the person carrying these bones?

I hear them whispering again

> *You **don't** deserve it*

> > ***No,** you don't deserve it*

mosaic of resilience

The light I carried through trauma

A soft glow of residual hope remaining

To build something new & meaningful

Still shines through the countless cracks

In my shattered soul – a mosaic of resilience

mosaic of resilience

I'm wondering – will it be enough?

To fight my demons that linger

Here in the darkness I created

Or were these succubi planted by

The vicious minds that hurt me?

SONGS OF

Magnolia Disorder

*"My brain is broken, tormented
by thoughts unspoken."*

disposable life

It's a disposable life I'm living

I'm not worth the fuss or thought

Just take what you need

And leave me behind

Like a coffee cup

Lined with potential

But nothing more

Than

A quick fix

You could get anywhere

disposable life

It's a disposable life I'm living

Yet I crave to be understood

Just so you'd know why

I am nothing

Covered in new skin

I carved on my own

In the darkest of times

When

My sick brain

Couldn't go anywhere

m a s s a c r e

I feel a song stinging under my skin

Inside my morbid soul, she's dreaming

A little girl's future in jeopardy

When there's nothing more than

Destruction and desolation

I feel the words flowing through my veins

Inside my rib cage, a demon screeching

It's fascinating how real my mind can feel

When I'm asked to choose between

A massacre and a memoir

crossed the line

All senses shut down by rage

I burst into flames, igniting

The curtains and carpets

My cranium torrid, tormented

Prisoner of my mind, I watch as I ignite

Once everything is scorched

I'm left with the fallout

All senses heightened

As I'm anxious to look

At the graveyard in front of me

ghosts of times past

For years I ignored my symptoms

Like I was completely fine

Thinking I was just lazy and dumb

Yet I was depressed & borderline

I've tried to erase my past

Like it never happened to me

But these wounds meant something

They still do to this day

ghosts of times past

II

They paint a picture of the

Complex trauma I endured for years

Each school day was a nightmare

A scar for every abuse

I was too weak to confront you

Too paralysed to ask for help

So I took all this hate I felt for you

And took it all out on myself

ghosts of times past

III

Now all that remains are the ruins

And a thousand scars on display

ghosts of times past

IV

My ghost of times past still beside me

A devil residing in my brain

tidal waves

I am all the emotions

A human can possibly feel

Like a tidal wave

Euphoria pumping through my veins

I'm okay

Then giving way to bottomless sorrow

I'm not okay

To the point of torpor

When I feel nothing at all

I am all the emotions

And none of them

dopamine

I sometimes trigger myself

I provoke these chemicals,

The rush of dopamine,

Like a whirlwind in my veins

It's better than feeling

Nothing at all, I guess;

I'm so borderline, it's crazy

It's like there's no other way

I cannot help but hide

So I keep the lid on

And bottle it all up nicely

Until I put on your song

And just crack with a pang;

A cycle I cannot escape

rotten

My mind is rotten

Like those pictures you've forgotten

Always anticipating the worst

Sending your venomous words

Directly to my heart with a knife

My brain is broken

Tormented by thoughts unspoken

Invisible, the demons hide

You can't accept what's out of sight

I wish I had just broken a bone

my mind's a wasteland

Words fail me, my mind is an abandoned ship

Nothing describes this void inside my chest

I'm hollow, as hollow as a tree long dead

And I alone reside in this cobwebbed vault

Desperately longing for an answer to unfold

For an antidote to chase away the nightmares

Haunting, scraping the insides of my skull

With their daunting fingers scooping sanity

How else to describe this overflowing emptiness?

the magician

I've got it all

Still, I'm not happy

That's the difference

Between you and me

Out of control

I burn it all down

That's the essence

Of my lunacy

the magician

Was it done to me?

Or did I create it myself?

The magician shapes

Her own deficiency

I'm grateful for you

The support that I need

Still, I'm grieving the lack

Of my independency

time's a thief

As the pendulum swings thoughtlessly

Oscillating to the rhythm of my heart

I eventually see time for what it really is:

Time's a thief, stealing valuable hours

Spent forlorn in a semiconscious stupor

Holding champagne memories prisoner

Never to see the light of day again

Time wasted on reckless behaviour

Making me think, is time the thief?

Or am I the one condemned to sabotage?

mausoleum

I hear their voices ringing in my ears

Howling, a heart desperate to express

Years of isolation, years of devastation

Have turned me into a mausoleum

Grenades detonating unexpectedly

On the bottom of what's left of me

I pick up the pieces, sharp & heavy

They cut into the flesh as I carry them

From disappointment to disappointment

Never allowed to rest & heal these wounds

Let them act as fertile soil for the flowers

Carelessly placed on my grave one day

distortion

I don't feel at home inside my head

And life's beginning to feel so surreal

It's alarming how different my mind feels

When my meds finally kick in

On good days, I tend to forget

The severity of the bad days I've had

And I start to question my madness

Was it all real? Am I a fraud?

distortion

II

What am I even complaining about?

I've got all I need to persist

It's amazing how my mind can distort things

To the point where I can't tell what's real

distortion

I

analyse

every

word

you

say

assuming

it's a

threat

III

amidst the storm

Bruises, self-inflicted madness

Screams echo through the halls

When I am pushed too far

I feel too much to process it all

In the end, it's always my fault

Paper skin surrenders to recoil

More damage done than intended

But less than in former times

It's all I can do to try and mend it

When I dance around the thunderbolt

adrenaline

These bruises remind me

That the pain was real

My soul was in flames

And I didn't see another way

When adrenaline hits you

Everything shuts off and

That's how I ended up here

And I love the colours

weighted blanket

These words are a blanket

A patchwork quilt of emotions

I sleep underneath, peacefully

A shelter for the inner child

Where I can speak my truth

Without their reckless stares

Gaping mouths laughing at me

I don't have to hide under stones

I am welcomed with open arms

These words are a blanket

And you can't hurt me anymore

my safe haven

No matter how painful

No matter how traumatic

The things you throw at me

I'll always have my imagination

My vast refuge, my safe haven

I can return to any time

In an instant, I dream up

Fairy tales & avid adventures

To protect myself from real life

That's become too much to take

So let me go, I don't belong here

Let me fly with the birds

Singing of happier times

back to normal

I've successfully unlearned

How to show true emotions

Lest they will hurt you

Lest they will hurt me

Shared pain is half the pain

Not for me, I'd feel it doubled

Double, double, toil & trouble

> *And it's already too much*
>
> For me alone to endure
>
> But you won't understand
>
> No one seems to understand
>
> And so I keep it to myself
>
> Waiting for sunnier days
>
> When everything's finally
>
> Back to normal

hiding in broad daylight

Maybe I had too much caffeine today

It would explain why I feel so odd

No words to describe this state of mind

I may need to cut back on black tea

And live in sombre, sober misery

It's not like I don't know my way around

The darkness that so easily finds me

In places I never thought it would look

hiding in broad daylight

For I am hiding in broad daylight

But where there's light, there are shadows

And they know my name by heart

Always ready to swallow me whole,

Those beasts have a stomach made of steel

And I cannot find my way out

to feel anything

If you had told me back then

That what I'm experiencing

Is nothingness in its purest form

I wouldn't have believed you

I guess I was so used to it

I didn't notice I was numb

But when I think about it now

I remember I used to hurt myself

To be able to cry and feel

To let it all out, the devastation;

Triggering myself on purpose

To show them this pain was real

As their words cut deep into my soul

leave / stay

And thus I find myself again in the shadows

It's warm & cosy here among the heartbreak

Like that's all I will ever feel and nothing less

I am the one who craved to be alone, so why

Do I feel abandoned by everyone around me?

Did I push you too far away to keep you here?

Have I finally reached the end of my sanity?

The air we breathe smothers me, yet I'll stay

I'm supposed to feel grateful, but I'm frozen

This winter will take the last of me, I'm so cold

the grim truth

It's a grim comfort knowing

If my world crumbles

There will be a way out

I feel at home among the words

She sang so beautifully

What I'm trying to say is

I built a boat out of these scars

A home among the tears

the grim truth

II

And should anything happen

The place I'll find myself in

Won't be unfamiliar

I know how to be alone

(It doesn't mean I want to)

This would be the end of me

Dependent on those around me

I will never grow up

I will never grow old

sevenfold

I carry the hate of seven within me

A volcano erupting unexpectedly

Demons pounding on the walls

Desperate attempts to make sense

Of the anger I feel over trivialities

My thoughts longing for silence

Let me calm down on my terms

I carry the love of seven within me

A plague of butterflies out of control

And there's nothing I can do about it

I have to learn to accept these beasts

To welcome them with open arms

And drown them in a lake of stupor

Where all my thoughts will go one day

in dissociation

I don't know what's wrong with me

Curled up in a ball, I freeze & shake

Memories come flashing back again

I turn into a helpless little child

How to help myself? I'm learning

It's a process, and I came here to write

To make sense of my traumatised mind

This weird thing interrupting my day

Don't forget to

breathe... breathe...

i'm fine

I'm done apologising

For saying I'm fine when I'm not

You have to understand

I'm more sensitive to emotions

I detect them from a mile away

So if I ruin the mood by being honest

And admit I've had a bad day

I feel the shift so intensely

It only makes things worse

i'm fine

For I feel everything so much stronger

Than you could ever imagine

So please, just let me deal with it

And trust that I won't unravel unnoticed

I've survived all of my bad days

I know when it gets too dark in here

And if it does, I promise you'll notice

For I'll be crying & screaming in the streets

To be noticed by absolutely everyone

achromatic tattoos

I don't know what you'll think of me

When I tell you that these scars are real,

Abundant metaphors for mental pain,

Manifested on my skin like invisible ink,

Became discernible under the torrid flame

Leaving me with these achromatic tattoos

Lacklustre remnants of self-inflicted carnage

So explicitly stating 'borderline'

I needed time to accept these cicatrices

But I am not ashamed anymore

thoughts on a bus

One thing I've wondered lately

When I'm on a bus in *s u m m e r*

Are they avoiding me, my arms?

Am I too ugly, too deranged?

And does it make a difference

When I'm on a bus in *w i n t e r?*

I can't look inside their skulls

But my mind has already

Created a story against myself

outside the movie set

In this movie you call my life

I've been promised the leading role

But you don't know my secret

I'm not the actress on the screen

But merely the camerawoman

Documenting a life interrupted

Powerlessly watching it go by

As I film every single memory

Blurry vision, stammered lines

I've recorded the worst of times

When all I want is to regain control

Over what cannot be controlled

manic pixie strange girl

A personality for every occasion

I slightly change based on how I feel:

On the movies I watch and

The music I listen to, they influence me

Just like the people that surround me

I can be so many things

The depressed girl in Victorian dress

Or the manic pixie dream girl

Dancing in the rain, laughing at the Sun

Making wishes upon the Moon

Still I haven't found the real me

expiration date

The outside pretends everything's fine

I am healed, I'm okay, I am resilient

But the inside is a decaying thing with

Rotten bones yearning so desperately

To be fixed, to be held, to be saved

How to repair the damage done?

My heart has reached its expiration date

And I'm ready to discard the carcass

Poisoning me all these wasted years

Living with a hole instead of a heart

Seems like the better option these days

At least then you'd know I'm not okay

pumpkin spice

You used the wrong jar of pumpkin spice

For your annual kitchen experiments

And I swear had I not been on medication

I would have broken down again

Instead, I accepted the hurt & the sadness

And poured it into this stupid poem

IV

SONGS OF

Lavender Sorrow

"Let poetry dress these wounds,
a magical world I can lose
myself in."

square one

The life I knew is gone

Now there's darkness

Encompassing me

Anywhere I go

To you, I appear normal

Like nothing's changed

I've learned to hide the pain

So long ago

But I am devastated

More than you'll ever know

Back to square one

With this endless sadness inside me

z o m b i e

I was alone when I got the news

I knew right then and there

That I was amidst the trauma

And that it would be a long way

Back to 'normal', I'm so *depressed*

I can't fathom the downhill ride

My life took when yours ended

I've become an empty shell

Lost in my own mind

There's no way out

darkness

The darkness has found me again

Slipped through a crack in the door

And seeped into my exhausted soul

While I was trying to hold it together

This darkness has infected me

Making me want to live in solitude

And do the things I've done before

Every thought poisoned & unrefined

My brain yet again my worst enemy

gift wrap

A secret hiding behind these eyes

I trembled as I smiled

The future I had pictured

Turned into bittersweet bile

A nightmare I'd never grasp

I knew about your twinship

As I stood and feigned surprise

I was left outside alone

To dissect my own demise

My pain concealed in gift wrap

I desperately wanted to be you

Naïve, happy, and whole

As I got one step closer

I was kicked down the rabbit hole

Waving my future adieu

halfway blooming

Springtime washed ashore

In colours of mint green

And pastel yellow hues

An idea as fragile as a

Sprout carefully grown

I felt the petals forming

Pigmented abundantly

halfway blooming

No need for those

Rose-coloured glasses

When everything aligns

In perfect harmony until

They ripped your heart out

Along with mine, viciously

I was halfway blooming

When the world

    just

        stopped

           spinning

peace from the fire

This heavy load on my shoulders pulls me down

To the slippery, crimson floor of despair

I can't help but feel lost inside these walls

Dragging myself from nightmare to nightmare

When all I want is peace from the fire

Burning a hole where my heart used to be

I'm a shell I cannot escape

four months later

The problem is that

Losing you was only the start

My grief has morphed into

Permanent heartache

And depression persists

Sticking like venomous syrup

In the middle of my sternum

Spreading to my limbs

Until I can barely breathe

And I slip into a dream

To soften the brutal blow

And I'm fine again for now

summer

Summer has been cancelled

Not only because

It's been raining for weeks

But also because

It never found its way

                Into my once budding heart

                With spring came life

                You gave me purpose

                You gave me hope

                It all swindled too soon

                And I'm left with

                Persistent winter in my heart

black

Black, as the colour of my soul

I feel like I'm forever broken

If my body isn't showing

At least the fabric says it all

I don't want to be so unhappy

I never chose this path for me

I just didn't see it coming

What else am I supposed to feel?

i'm a prisoner

I just can't help but feel miserable

There's a heaviness in my throat

A crumbling heart-shaped stone

Yearning for deliverance

No matter how much I toss & turn

There's just no way out of this

All I can do is survive & smile

While my soul slowly deteriorates

heavy clouds

I've come to love the rain at night

As I've used up this year's supply

Of tears to cry, to soak this mask

That I carried with me every time

The pain was mine alone to feel

        And I slowly watched my life unravel

        These days, there's only nothingness

        And passive I watch the heavy clouds

        Shed their worries – an exhale

        To breathe in new hope

        Soothing droplets on my skylight

        I've come to love the rain at night

        For it has taught me at least this much

extinguished heart

I imagine the sky is crying for me

Big saline drops of despair I've shed

On the floor, defeated, paralysed

My whole body hurting, the shock

Of realising I'm not getting better

Even on anti-depressants, I'm ablaze

I've lost myself inside myself

Detached, from a distance, torpid

I watch your life unfold in front of me

And all that's left are desolate cinders

A flickering heart extinguished

By the sky crying with me

to bury a child

Today's the day I'll bury my child

It's been five months now

And to be honest,

I'm not as heartbroken anymore

I mourn different things now

Like, why is there no rainbow in sight?

While everyone around me is blessed

Whatever little strength was left in me

I've lost it along the way

And I don't believe in hope anymore

It's a cruel thing keeping me awake

It's eating away at my heart

I want to break away

world of poetry

I want these words to fill me up

Until there's no more space

For this pain, tearing me apart

I need something to numb this grief

Let poetry dress these wounds

A magical world I can lose myself in

When everything turns to dust around me

I want these words to stop the tears

And let hope back into my heart

Because I can only bleed so much

Until there's nothing left anymore

Let the ink flow down these pages

I want to get lost in this pool of letters

an unspoken virtue

Some waves of mourning cry beyond the moment

Leaving me in a state of torpor, an opaque fog rising

A beating heart irretrievably lost in fantastical realms

Where love's a disease and grief an unspoken virtue

Granted to those only who have suffered the most

No new dawn for the languidly decaying souls of yore

On the horizon, a thin veil of remembrance remains

first day of spring

On the first day of spring

I don't feel it at all

It's not even the weather

There's still winter in my heart

Still lingering, still hurting

I will forever mourn your passing

You being alive –

Had always been a symbol of hope

That we can make it

Despite what life throws at us

first day of spring

You being gone –

Only proves one thing

I've got no one left in my corner

No one like me, no one like me

If only you could look and see

How I'm still fighting for life

In a world without you in it

pot of honey

There can be no doubt

The roses are fading

Their colour is vanishing

Their scent evaporating

Their thorns sharpening

As I look the other way

Everything is ever-changing

So I take my pot of honey

And these wilted petals

For I'm trying to reunite

The petal and the pedicel

A pointless endeavour

Yet, please, let me try

I'm not ready to let go

transformation

I'm sorry I've become too dark for you

All black hearts and morbid jokes

I'm sorry I returned to what I've known

The music and the clothes I wear

It's all so familiar, and I don't mind

You can plead as much as you want

I will not go back to who I was

That person died in lonely grief

When the pandemic took so much

if i had a heart

I guess it's no secret, the ultrasound

Proves what I already knew:

There's a hole in my chest

Maybe when I had the surgery

They removed more than my baby

Where once two hearts beat

Now remains a deafening silence

I haven't been myself ever since

And you wonder why I'm so cold

What they simply don't get is

This changed me, the old me

Irrevocably lost in the exam room

midnight at the graveyard

The cold air chills me to the bones

I'm frozen in time among the dead

All these lives lived and irretrievably lost

Resting in peace in sacred earth

Nothing can stir their heavy sleep

 Despite the frost, I look for your grave

 Your name in bold letters inscribed

 On the tombstone unmistakably yours

 I'll sit with you for a while, my dear

 And lay a white rose soaked in tears

  The clock strikes twelve, startling me

  As I tell you how sorry I am, even though

  There is nothing that I could have done

  You were important, you are missed

  And it hurts that I never told you that

heartbroken

The room smells like shock and grief

And I admit, I'm still in disbelief

This cannot be my new reality

I'm spiralling into insanity

But it's so difficult to say your name

Or listen to your voice

I'm shattered and I'm hopeless

I don't know how to fix this

I don't want this to be the new status quo

I want to push it away, I cannot let go

There wasn't a day this past fortnight

I didn't start crying, I'm not all right

heartbroken

A whole year I wasted, avoiding the truth

Now I see that I just have to pull through

Open up and come to terms with the fact

That I'm hurting so much, I'm scared to react

Shocked and heartbroken, because it's true

I've become a master in avoiding

All thoughts about you

And it's tearing me apart

That you will never know

in a lavender field near necropolis

We catch ghosts like fireflies

In a lavender field near Necropolis

To keep your memory alive

In a small jar made of clear glass

We hold on to a past once tangible

As we walk along this pebbled path

Change palpable under our feet

A future we claim with every step

It misses the contours of your skin

Now spectral vapours preserved

Like the taste of sweet summer berries

The air that once graced your lungs

Seeps through our trembling hands

Into a small jar made for memories

kaleidoscope

Last spring, my heart bloomed beautifully

Then darkness came, ferocious beast

I watched in horror as my world caved in

The sudden shock left me colour-blind

To summer's blossoms & buoyancy

I hope this time it will be different

Rediscovering life in kaleidoscopic bloom

victory

Every day is a victory

With the hours passing by

We get closer to a future

That wasn't meant to be

We get closer to the rainbow

I so desperately want to see

Every smile is a victory

Please keep reminding me

There's beauty in the pain

Not a lesson to be learned

There's beauty in the suffering

These battle scars I earned

roller coaster world

Something's lurking in the shadows

A dewy vapour of all my past mistakes

Lingering on the constantly doubtful mind

Trying to make sense of the trauma

As if there would ever be any answers

To the questions no one dared to ask

It's a roller coaster world I live in

And I've come to realise that

Nothing makes sense anymore

the secret garden

Seasons change and so do I

Competing with the flowers in spring

I grew a beautiful yet secret garden

But as soon as I'd let anyone in

The flowers withered & turned to dust

What followed was persistent summer rain

Only now that everything is dying

I feel at home in my skin again

And there's comfort in knowing

There will be another spring for me

• A TANKA •

honeysuckle hope

Honeysuckle hope

It took me on a journey

A land of promise

It was not my path to take

To taste a daydream's sweetness

drop by drop

Rain, wash away these memories

That keep resurfacing at midnight

It's pouring and I love the sound

Drowning out the noise in my head

Drop by drop, tapping on my window

A soothing melody for the broken

To make those forgotten flowers bloom

Sleepy seeds lingering in the cracks

Rain, wash away this uncertainty

ebon diamond

I still hold anger in my heart

Like a treasured ebon diamond

Teach me how to let go of this

I'm tired of feeling so sullen

Let hope grow like wildflowers

And weave them into a crown

To place upon this heavy head

I am the queen of perseverance

I can't escape these silver chains

Tying me to tomorrow's rain

You'll find me on sodden ground

As I pray for a sliver of sunlight

thoughts on a new moon

My heart is as cold & dark as the New Moon

No light at the end of the tunnel for me

This path is never-ending, where will it lead me?

thoughts on a new moon

II

But hope keeps reappearing like a Full Moon

Holding me prisoner until the crack of dawn

When frustration sets in and dreams die

This pain is never-ending, when will it stop?

SONGS OF

Cerulean Misery

"*Heartbroken, I sit surrounded
by poems that won't ever
make any sense to you.*"

sleep after the storm

It's getting worse and worse

Nowhere to turn to, trapped in a train

Of thought that's driving me mad

I try to be clever and try something new

But I escalate into panic mode

I knew I was going to end up in a hospital

Because I can't hold myself together

And I have no future

I rage and I react and I panic and I hurt

sleep after the storm

Something to calm the nerves is nice

I feel dazed and tired, but most of all

I don't worry about every single thing

Every thought I start dissolves

Into *nothingness*, I can't remember

I'm not shaking anymore

I'm calm and I'm numb and I'm all right

It's bliss

bitter things

Like black coffee on an empty stomach

Grapefruit juice when you expected orange

My anxiety pills on my tongue like candy

Slowly dissolving into nothingness

I'm all the bitter things

Keeping me on edge, spitting bile

The venom in my veins infecting

So many innocent lives, I've lost count

How to purge this madness

Flowing underneath my corroded skin

don't forget to breathe

I remember that one winter

When I wasn't able to breathe

Stuck underwater without knowing

Where all of this was coming from

I felt a brick in my neck & lungs

No oxygen or cause was to be found

I held my breath for several months

Popping pills in the emergency room

Until my therapist figured it out:

I was suffering from panic attacks

And being off my meds didn't help

an open book

It takes a special kind of courage

To be this vulnerable in the spotlight

I admire you for your bravery

And I wish I could follow in your footsteps

But this anxiety's holding me back

Pair that with perfectionism

The perfect storm for failure

Will I ever achieve anything?

Where is this road leading me?

iridescent

A plunge into the unknown

I seek the iridescent light

Glistening in the distance

Too late to change my mind

This fear is slowly creeping

An obstacle I can't face

To live means to ignore it

And go at my own pace

anyway

Hold your breath they said

To keep yourself from crying

Because crying's not allowed here

Calm down

Count to ten they said

And everything will be all right

Because screaming's not an option

Calm down

anyway

Get over it they said

Everyone's sad at times

Because that's just life, so

Calm down

And I cry anyway

(Tears flowing uncontrollably)

And I scream anyway

(Trying to get rid of the pain)

And I hurt anyway

(Because nothing's helping)

boundaries

The truth is plain & simple

I don't set boundaries

It's so hard for me to say 'no'

Because I don't want you to

Be disappointed in me

And then subliminally hate me

Add to that spontaneity

To make a perfect mess

Because I can say 'yes' faster

Than my anxious brain can fret

overwhelmed

It's the tiny things that overwhelm me

In times like these

Like combing my hair and taking my pills

I'm scared it will be like this forever

It just doesn't go away

The stress I feel to do

Everything at *once*

And so sometimes I end up doing

Nothing at *all*

mindfulness

Agitated, irritable, I try to focus

But I'm bubbling on the inside

Like a soda bottle about to burst

There's still so much to do

The tension in the back of my head

Keeps nagging at me continuously

I need to take better care of me

It sounds easy, but I'm clueless

When was the last time I took

A deep breath and let it all go?

the dragon

Oh God, what am I doing?

I can't go down this road again

Yet here I am, halfway burned

From excruciating flames

This dragon inside me

Guarding my heart of coal

It's burning slowly to the ground

When this is all over

I'll be left with nothing

I want to escape from here

safety plan

I have to accept the fact

That I'm depressed again

It's so obvious

I saw the signs and ignored them

Thinking I'm just grieving

But again I feel this brick

Inside my chest, preventing me

From getting out of bed today

And doing the things I like to do

My brain turned into a beast

Out to get me at every turn

Trying to convince me

I'm a burden; and your life

Would be better without me

safety plan

But I'm more aware now than I used to

And I took the right precautions

I've got a safety plan in place

I'll be fine

I'll be fine

haunted

Haunted by panic attacks, I get through the day

Praying for my pounding heart not to explode

My hands are shaking, my mind's in a daze

Always on the lookout, I watch my life unravel

I don't know how to fix myself, but I'm trying

When did happiness leave my soul, I wonder?

Will everything turn out all right in the end?

I'm a bag of bones & burden, and a heavy heart

Doubt is my best friend, following me around

Haunted by anxiety, I still keep moving on

honest

I'm fine with what I've shared

Yet anxiety rears its ugly head

Every once in a while, but

This is my chance to prove

That I can bear your eyes

On the very words

Residing in my mind

You either get all of me

Or nothing at all anymore

stir crazy

The things you experience in lockdown

I never thought possible, yet here I am

Heartbroken, I sit surrounded by poems

That won't ever make any sense to you

I don't know what is happening to me

Am I going stir crazy? Or just insane?

The latter is easier to manage, I suppose

There are a million things left to say

But so little space to spill these beans

That linger around my mind, sprouting

Maybe one day I'll find those golden eggs

thoughts on a full moon, pt. I

The rain dances on the windowpane

I haven't felt this calm in a long while

Was that the magic trick all along?

Increasing the dose of my medication

To rid myself of this nagging anxiety?

I pray to the gods that this will last

I'm sick of being depressed & anxious

With so much on my mind, I didn't see

The life I get to live despite everything

Yes, this tightness behind my ribs is gone

And I can finally breathe again

Please, let this be the start of something

Good; on this Full Moon, I sit & hope

SONGS OF

Emerald Hope

*"A bed of delicate flowers to rest
my heavy heart when darkness
remains all-consuming, dreary."*

s h o c k

My mind works in mysterious ways

It's honest and ashamed

This is my new identity

For you to meet again

Things I don't usually talk about

My therapist has no clue

But every poem's a part of me

A scar I can't undo

It's painful for you and me to observe

But I'll rise again one day

From the ashes as in mythology

Of the bridges I burned today

bird's eye view

I know I'm broken, but

Only I can fix myself

So I take these words

And make them mine

A delicate web of phrases

Tightly knit together

To mend these ruptured wings

So one day, I may rise

And soar towards the sky

To get a bird's eye view

Of this life I call my own

s e m i c o l o n

Against all odds

I'm still here

Who'd have thought?

I still breathe

;

Against all odds

I survived

My darkest days

And longest nights

semicolon

In disbelief

I look at you

Asking silently

Am I enough?

;

A semicolon

On my brain

I will die

But not today

let me bloom

Let me bloom as flowers do

Even as the days grow colder

And the leaves find it hard to

Hold onto these brittle branches

I am not a delicate flower, no

I am the weeds under your porch

And I will not stop growing until

Crimson petals sprout from these bones

For every scar earned & battle fought

    Let

        me

           bloom

the dance of autumn

Is this the end or a new beginning?

When everything around me is dying

Will it make room for something novel?

I'm yearning for transformation

If the leaves can change, so can I

You'll find me sitting under a tree

In all of autumn's vibrant colours

Ready for another facet of my life

I will dance among the leaves in the wind

One with nature, I will reach new heights

peace of mind

Curiosity killed the cat

But it won't kill me

On the contrary

It keeps me alive

Always curious about

What tomorrow may bring

And I won't lay down this pen

Capturing a life

I've lived the best I could

Yes, it's been rough

It still is most days

But every day I wake up

And face the storm

Over and over again

With confidence that

I'll find my peace of mind

time to heal

I don't want you to worry

Or to feel uncomfortable

So I lie and I say everything's good

It helps me to forget for a while

To distract from the grief

That I feel every day, you know why

I can't tell you when I'll be better

But I hope it won't be long

I think my pills are finally working

Give me time

I need time

a garden for the heavy heart

Memories stream

Down this pallid face

A serenade of drops

Descending to the ground

Watering the seeds

I sowed on a New Moon

Hopefully, growing into

Precious flowers one day:

Azaleas of Acceptance,

Hydrangeas of Hope,

Sunflowers of Solace

A bed of delicate flowers

To rest my heavy heart

When darkness remains

All-consuming, dreary

These blossoms will be

My guiding light, I pray

sigh of relief

It's like this year is ending

With a great sigh of relief

We've been through so much

Hitting the point where

It couldn't get any worse

So it got better instead

Desperate for good news

They slowly trickled in

Making room in my heart

For hope & confidence

That everything will be okay

moment of clarity

In this moment of clarity

I feel free, I feel fine

At peace with my thoughts

I draw outside the lines

Aware of my accomplishments

I look up to the sun

Striving in the bright light

It's not over, I'm not done

i will find a way

I will find a way

I just need to remember

To *b r e a t h e...*

I will find a way

This might not seem ideal

I'm a complete mess

But I will find a way

It may cost a broken bone

(But who says

It has to be mine?)

I will find a way

I will be okay, I know

Everything will be fine

I may get out of this

A l i v e

thoughts on a full moon, pt. II

Another Full Moon has arrived tonight

Illuminating the darkness under my skin

As the Moon travels the starry night sky

I feel wide awake & bursting with potential

All the legends & sagas I could write tonight

Ideas floating around my mind like dragonflies

I miss the spark that sets it all on fire

Unburdened, weightless, I'd start from scratch

Painting a perfect version of myself, untainted

In the silent moonlight shining on the lake

I'd sit there and write of rainbows & færies

A life I long to create someday

these hands

These hands have done many a deed

They held the knife that cut my soul

They hit the walls that held me close

They played the keys to tunes of hope

Wrapped around the harshness of grief

These hands have written many a letter

Addressed to an illiterate heart of stone

Yet they don't surrender to the weight

Placed upon these upturned palms

• A SHAKESPEAREAN SONNET •

underneath the starlit sky

I'd love to hold these stars close to my heart

Each one a memory I want to keep

To shine a light when it gets cold and dark

When wolves roam among the counted sheep

And as the Moon perdures to wax and wane

I search for answers buried deep within

To get a sense of what will soon remain

Of all the nightmares underneath my skin

• A SHAKESPEAREAN SONNET •

underneath the starlit sky

II

Tonight I'll look for magic in the trees

Among the shooting stars & fireflies

I'll catch a glimpse of all the might-have-beens

Determined to ignore the siren's cries

To live a life with moonlight on my mind

In hope of finding grace in humankind

• **A TANKA** •

a light in the dark

A light in the dark

Glistening through broken glass

Distorted yet bright

Curious glances reveal

Not all hope is lost tonight

Thank you for reading.

Notes & Credits

The First Line Poets project hosted by **Emma-Jane Barlow** (*@emmajanepoetry*) on Instagram has allowed me to challenge my creativity in new and exciting ways.

I've been given many great first lines by amazing poets which inspired the poems in this collection on the following page.

Thank you to the editors of the following journal in which the poem "Distorted Glass" first appeared:

Eve Poetry Magazine

Notes & Credits

"An Unspoken Virtue"
was inspired by
Stuti (IG: *@weavingtapestry*)

"Pot of Honey"
was inspired by
Ted (IG: *@a_buddhas_pen*)

"In a Lavender Field Near Necropolis"
was inspired by
Ginger (IG: *@ayla.poetry*)

Acknowledgements

First and foremost, I would love to thank Ralf for being my rock during these difficult times, for giving me the space to express myself, and for letting me release my creativity. Your support means the world to me.

I cannot express enough thanks to Brooke for editing this poetry collection. Your feedback proved invaluable and I cannot thank you enough!

And of course, a huge thank you to Beth for bringing my vision of the cover and interior design of this book to life. Thank you so much!

Furthermore, I am so thankful to Ada for your constructive criticism, as well as your friendship. I'm also extremely grateful to my dear friends, Aubree & Kim, for reading early drafts and for providing helpful feedback when I was doubting myself. Without you, I wouldn't have had the courage to publish this at all. Thank you for accepting my darkness and making me feel heard.

Lastly, I'd love to thank you for reading this book you're holding in your hands. I'm so grateful to each and every one of you for your support. Thank you!

About the Author

Serena Morrigan is a writer and mental health advocate hoping to end the stigma one poem at a time. She studied English and Japanese at university, but eventually set her focus on writing poetry, something that gives her a sense of purpose.

Her work has been published in several print and online publications, including *Train River*, and *Eve Poetry Magazine*. She is a member of the collaborative *First Line Poets project*. Find Serena's, as well as others' collaborations on Instagram: *@firstlinepoets*

For more of Serena's work, find her on Instagram: *@Serena.Morrigan*